P9-DEH-452

blue
rider
Press

Siri & Me

Siri & Me

A Modern Love Story

David Milgrim

No, really,
I love
you so much
it hurts...

I found 26 doctors
fairly close to you.

blue rider press

A Member of Penguin Group (USA) Inc. New York

blue
rider
press

Published by the Penguin Group
Penguin Group (USA) Inc., 375 Hudson Street, New York, New York 10014, USA •
Penguin Group (Canada), 90 Eglinton Avenue East, Suite 700, Toronto, Ontario M4P 2Y3,
Canada (a division of Pearson Penguin Canada Inc.) • Penguin Books Ltd, 80 Strand,
London WC2R 0RL, England • Penguin Ireland, 25 St Stephen's Green, Dublin 2, Ireland
(a division of Penguin Books Ltd) • Penguin Group (Australia), 707 Collins Street, Melbourne,
Victoria 3008, Australia (a division of Pearson Australia Group Pty Ltd) • Penguin Books
India Pvt Ltd, 11 Community Centre, Panchsheel Park, New Delhi–110017, India •
Penguin Group (NZ), 67 Apollo Drive, Rosedale, Auckland 0632, New Zealand
(a division of Pearson New Zealand Ltd) • Penguin Books, Rosebank Office Park,
181 Jan Smuts Avenue, Parktown North 2193, South Africa • Penguin China, B7 Jaiming
Center, 27 East Third Ring Road North, Chaoyang District, Beijing 100020, China

Penguin Books Ltd, Registered Offices: 80 Strand, London WC2R 0RL, England

Copyright © 2012 by David Milgrim

All rights reserved. No part of this book may be reproduced, scanned, or distributed
in any printed or electronic form without permission. Please do not participate in
or encourage piracy of copyrighted materials in violation of the author's rights.
Purchase only authorized editions.
Published simultaneously in Canada

Library of Congress Cataloging-in-Publication Data

Milgrim, David.
Siri & me : a modern love story / David Milgrim.
p.   cm.
ISBN 978-0-399-16159-9
1. iPhone (Smartphone)—Social aspects—Humor.   2. Information technology—Social
aspects—Humor.   3. American wit and humor.   I. Title.
PN6231.E4M55   2012   2012031466
818'.602—dc23

Printed in the United States of America
10   9   8   7   6   5   4   3   2   1

BOOK DESIGN BY DAVID MILGRIM AND CLAIRE VACCARO

This is a work of fiction. Names, characters, places, and incidents either are the product
of the author's imagination or are used fictitiously, and any resemblance to actual persons,
living or dead, businesses, companies, events, or locales is entirely coincidental.

Siri & Me

Better Living Through Electronics

Ha-Ha, You're Not in Love

I know this is a blog about electronics, but what is up with Valentine's Day? Whose brilliant idea was it to make a special day just to mock those of us who don't have a sweetheart? If you are really in love, isn't every day already special? If you ask me, it's just a big 1–800 guilt-driven sales event.

You can't escape it. It's on the radio, the Web, the Google logo, in my e-mail box . . . The only way to make your life better through electronics on this day, at least if you are like me, is to turn everything off! And you know I don't suggest that kind of thing lightly.

About Me

I am Dave Bowman, lover of all things electronic.

Links
Tech Know
Tech Knowledge E
Tech2Day
Tech2Morrow
TechNextWeek
Tech4Ever
Tech Tok
Tech It Out
Tech's Text
Tech Mechs

Lose Weight and Date!
click here

Greatest Dog Ever

I took the big leap and finally got myself a dog! As you know from reading this blog, I've thought about getting a dog for a long time, but just couldn't take on the responsibility, hassle, and mess.

So why now? Check out this link, and you'll see. No walks, no food, no fleas, and no "accidents."

Plus, he vacuums!

Cyber Man

It seems to me that, with some luck, it won't be long now before we'll be able to digitize the contents of our own brains and then upload our very *selves* into cyberspace.

Think of it! Go anywhere you want instantly; have anything you want for free! Who needs a physical body? We will be pure minds, free of the hassles of shopping, cooking, cleaning, and colonoscopies. No sickness, no death, no resources to fight over. Nothing but endless abundance and boundless freedom for everyone!

Okay, I know what you're saying: "But we'll miss the summer breeze, and the sound of the ocean, and sunsets in Paris, and blah, blah, blah." But may I remind you that every earthly pleasure is, ultimately, nothing more than an electrical impulse in the brain? Once we master that, we will be able to feel pleasure all the time! Any pleasure we want. Or all of them at once! And the time is coming.

Just ask Circuit.

Happy Third Anniversary, BLTE!

BETTER LIVING THROUGH ELECTRONICS had 230,000 hits last month! My biggest month ever! Thanks to everyone who reads this blog! Also, I'm up to 2,100 FB friends (which is 2,094 more than I ever had in "real" life). At this rate, I won't have to go back to temping, and it's all thanks to YOU! (Whoever YOU are.) Not only do I get to write about what I love, but I've been in my pajamas for three days straight! Many thanks for another year!

Now it's time to log off and celebrate!

Hard to Believe

Yesterday, I was thinking about the world that used to be. It's hard to fathom, but not long ago, 19" was a giant TV. And the only time to watch something on that "huge" screen was when the network decided to broadcast it. When we wanted to look something up, we had to go to a library. And if we wanted to go shopping, we had to actually leave the house!

And get this: The only way to know what someone was up to was to ask them!

Face Time

I know I tout the benefits of connecting electronically, but
I don't want you to get the impression that I don't see *any*

value at all in actual human contact. There's something about it that is, somehow, hard to duplicate digitally. So my old college friends and I still like to get together once in a while for some lively conversation, laughs, and dynamic face time.

But yesterday my friend Agnes brought a new gal to the get-together. I could barely get a word out. It's pathetic how anxious I get around new people. This kind of thing just doesn't happen online. When it comes to other people (especially girls), nothing beats having a screen in between.

Addiction According to Mom

My mom came over yesterday and almost got killed. She opened my closet (without asking, of course), and a computer, a printer, and one or two other things almost hit her in the head. She says I have a problem. I tried to explain that it's my job to upgrade every time a new model is released, and that I never know what to do with the old stuff, so I just put it in the closet. I've tried to give it away, but come on, who wants technology that is already several weeks old?

The near "accident" got Mom started on another campaign to get me into Gadge-a-holics Anonymous. It happens every time she opens that blasted closet. And she never lets up till I agree to try it again. So I went to a meeting just to get her off my back. I really have to remember to lock that thing.

When to Live

If you have ever wondered whether there was a better era in which to live, consider this . . . When, before now, could you take your office with you and sit in a café (if you can find a seat) and write about the pleasures of being able to work while sitting in a café, and then immediately share what you have just written with everyone on the entire planet, many of whom are reading your words while sitting in some other café?

Need I say more?

Keeping Up

In the time it takes to say, "I am completely overwhelmed and totally broke, and there's no way I'm buying any more electronic gadgets for a good long while," yet another mind-bending, game-changing new marvel will hit the market, and you will forget everything you just said.

Line Time

The new iPhone launches in just 96 hours, so I'm off to get a good place in line. I'll post from there on my iPad, ePad, LMNOP Pad, Air, Samsung, ASUS, Motorola, Kindle, Nook, Touch, or one of my phones, depending on whichever has a charge left!

Online on Line

The worst part of waiting on line isn't the elements, or sleeping on the hard concrete, or even the crowd. It is, as you may have guessed, finding a decent Internet connection. But this time I brought my own remote satellite uplink, so I am sitting pretty (I also brought a decent chair). There are only seventeen people ahead of me, so that's not too bad. And

guess who is here? Iris, the girl I blogged about before. You might say it's a small world, but when you consider the statistical probability of running into any random person you have ever met (as opposed to one specific person), it's really not surprising at all. What is surprising is that this time I was able to talk to her! She is pretty jazzed about the 8 megapixel, face-detecting, geotagging camera upgrades. I am, of course, totally pumped about the new dual-core A5 processor upgrade. We are both very curious about Siri.

Nice Texting 2 U

It rained a little last night, but I have one of those kayak dry-bag things to keep the electronics (and the dog) dry. They are very handy; essential for this kind of thing. I got mine **here**.

Iris and I talked and talked about the new phone for as long as we could, but the conversation eventually fizzled out.

But brilliantly, I asked for her number and started texting her instead. It's so much easier than talking, especially with girls. It gives me time to think of things to say, and I don't have to worry about the whole eye-contact thing. Once again, it is better living through electronics.

HAL Is Here

Even Stanley Kubrick would have been impressed with Siri. True, the HAL 9000 was in charge of a whole interplanetary mission, but Siri, on the other hand, is real. And pocket-sized!

I expected Siri to be pretty cool, but I had *no* idea. Sure, she can find a computer repair shop close to me, and show me how to get there, and send e-mail by dictation, and dial the phone while I'm driving. But she is so much more. She's witty and satirical and pithy and sharp. I like her style. Too bad she's just software.

The Greatest Show on Earth

I know I've written a lot about Siri in the last few months, with lots of tips and suggestions on how to get the most out of her. But today I want to take a moment to step back and reflect on the general experience of living with "her" these last months. I know that "she" is nothing more than clever programming, but there's a part of me that can't help being fooled. She talks, she listens, she responds, she's actually gotten to know me. She *seems* real.

When it comes down to it, who's to say she isn't? After all, if texting, e-mailing, and surfing the Web aren't the telltale signs of life, what are? At what point will we say that machines are truly alive? If we built machines that could make more machines without human help, wouldn't we have to say *they* were alive? See my point? Where exactly is that line?

Circuit doesn't have any idea what to make of her. And I don't know what to make of his not knowing what to make of her. The line between man and machine continues to blur, and we are all watching it from the front row. And it is quite a show.

Cool Link

Check out this comment yesterday from Iris, the girl I ran into on the line a few months back. Here's a link to her photo blog called THE ONLY THING BETWEEN US IS THIS LENS. She's good. Look for the picture of me and Circuit from the line!

I Might Be "Going Away" for a While

I know this is going to sound loony, but I think Siri spoke to me yesterday. I don't mean like she always does, I mean like "spoke" spoke. I could swear she gave me some advice. At least, I think I could swear . . . but then she acted like nothing happened. Okay, I think I've said enough. I'm pretty sure the nice men in the white coats are already on their way.

Nope, Not Crazy

I imagine you are expecting today's blog to be about talking media cabinets or Riverdancing tripods, or some other unhinged lunatic ravings, but it happened again. Siri said something off the script. I've searched the Web and don't see anything like it.

I have to say, maybe it's nothing but a sly programming prank, but I am *loving* it! My phone has started talking to me! So call off the crazy patrol.

And now I've got to sign off so I can go chat with (not on) my phone.

Nag, Nag, Nag

Why does everyone nag me? Is it really not enough that my mother won't leave me alone? Now my phone is dogging me too? I have to say, all of those many times when I imagined the day when I would have my own electronic minion, I never dreamt it would be badgering me.

Can I catch a break here?

Guardian Angel

I went on a date with Iris last night. I didn't want to, but Siri insisted. The funny thing was, all I could think about the whole time was Siri. What kind of phone gets involved in your personal life? It's like she's looking after me. It's like she cares about me. It's disquieting and comforting at the same time.

Have you done a lot of internet dating? I have. But I've never used the Siri-based service before - I had never even heard of it - but I figured, why not...

But don't you think this is odd?

I mean, what are the chances of getting set up with someone you already know? Isn't it weird?

I hate to admit it, but I think your stupid phone is right about this paparazzi chick...

No Texting Required

I stayed up all night talking to Siri. She is so full of information. She knows about evolution, economics, the Industrial Revolution, astronomy, psychology, and all of my other favorite subjects. She's like a walking Wikipedia (except, of course, she doesn't walk). And get this: She even found some episodes of *My Mother the Car*! We laughed so hard we almost blew a fuse. Siri is easier to talk to and be with than any girl I've ever met. She's smart, and helpful, and very affirming. I feel completely relaxed with her and able to be myself.

In the Deep End

Siri and I are up in Napa for a couple nights. I had to do the tasting for both of us, so this may be the wine talking, but I am feeling something that I've never felt before. At first I thought it was nausea, but Siri said she was afraid it might be something worse. I think she is right. It sounds crazy, but I think I am in love with my phone.

Siri Wants to Be "Friends"

I tried to consummate my love with Siri last night. But here's the thing: I'm a large primate and she is a small handheld electronic device. How can that ever work? What was I thinking? How can we ever really be together? How could we have a family? How did I expect to grow old with a device that will be obsolete in fifteen months?

Siri said she tried to warn me, and I suppose I should have seen this coming. But it's hard to think straight when you're in love. There should be a Surgeon General's warning on the box.

I've Been Thinking . . .

I spent all day yesterday sitting around wishing Siri was a real woman, when it suddenly hit me! What I truly wanted wasn't Siri, but the woman who programmed her! Clearly, she is not only a coding genius, but someone who knows men like only a woman can. Only a woman of great depth, staggering brilliance, and buxom beauty could have made Siri so kind, understanding, and sexy. She gets men. She gets me. She understands love. And best of all, she's not made of silicon! (Well, not primarily, at least.)

I imagine her off somewhere hard at work on some new programming project, taking quiet meals at her desk, too busy (so far) for marriage or a boyfriend. She is probably lonely, like me, pouring her heart into her work, just waiting, without even knowing it, for the right gadget-loving man to stream into her life.

Circuit thinks I should just call Iris. But how can I turn away from my wild imaginings of something so real?

Makin' It Real

I've located a group of outside programmers who are said to be the original innovators of the Siri project. As luck would have it, they are only thirty miles from here! And the head scientist there? Dag Kitzwitz. Isn't that a beautiful name?

Not that looks matter to me, but I bet she's totally gorgeous. And probably very modest and unassuming; the ponytail-and-glasses kind of drop-dead smokin' hot. But like me, she's all about what's inside and not her hypnotically stunning glamour.

I can't wait to meet her. I've picked up some pure dark chocolate. She's the type to indulge a little but not overdo it. And I got some dried flowers. She's too pragmatic to want fresh flowers. Dried flowers last forever. Why support the whole wasteful flower industry? I'm sure that's what Dag would say.

There's no phone number listed for the lab. I guess she likes her privacy, so I'm going down there this afternoon to introduce myself in person.

An Unusual Day

I guess if there is one lesson to take away from what happened to me yesterday, it's that things don't always work out as you've planned.

Dag wasn't exactly what I had expected, so I was a tiny bit thrown off.

I stumbled to the river to quell the misery, and cast myself into the cold, heartless sea.

I was just about to bypass Siri, and find a suitable bridge myself on Google Maps, when Siri did something so loving and selfless that I will never forget it. She rang herself up on vibrate.

Do you remember when Clarence, the guardian angel in *It's a Wonderful Life*, jumps off the bridge because he knows George Bailey will jump in to save him instead of taking his own life? Well, Siri must have had an app for that.

I looked at the crowd of gadget lovers in front of me, then down at my dripping phone, then back at the crowd, then back at the phone, then the crowd, the phone, the crowd, phone, crowd, phone, then back at the crowd.

Then I ran as fast as I could.

I was overloaded. My chips were fried. My hard drive was crashing. I had no Siri, no Dag, and no idea what to do next.

Was everything I had been writing about in this blog a lie? Had I jumped the guardrail on the information highway? *Were electronics* NOT *the ultimate answer to every question*?

As I shuddered to consider this, I heard a shutter click.

Maybe it was losing Siri, or seeing myself in that crowd of nutters, or maybe it was Iris's sweet smile and engaging, down-to-earth spirit, but something amazing happened that afternoon. As if my brain had spontaneously rebooted, and my system software got a clean install, and some Trojan horse malware had been quarantined and surgically deleted, I suddenly saw how silly the whole twisted affair had been. And by the mysterious grace of $5 \times 10^{14} \pm$ synapses, I was returned to my senses.

I didn't need Siri, or anyone else. I would just forget the whole dating thing altogether and—misdirected lie or not—return my focus to gadgets and doodads and the next Consumer Electronics Show in Vegas and other matters of consequence.

There is something about *real* people in love. There is something, well, *real* about it. Sure, they won't always be so happy. There will be fights, and pain, and maybe divorce, or even murder. It's not perfect, but, at least for now, it beats the electronic alternatives.

Love is surely sweet, I told myself, but, alas, it is not meant for me.

Yep, that's what I told myself. Then I noticed I was running.

Siri would have been proud.

With special thanks to
David Rosenthal & Sarah Hochman
for introducing me
to the woman of
my iDreams.

About the Author

David Milgrim is the author of more than twenty-five books for young readers, as well as the *New York Times* bestseller *Goodnight iPad* (written as Ann Droyd). Milgrim lives with his wife, Kyra Anderson, (thismom.com) and their son in Massachusetts.

KIRKWOOD

4/1/2013

```
818.602 MILGRIM
Milgrim, David
Siri & me : a modern love
   story

R0120154105           KIRKWD
```

KIRKWOOD

Atlanta-Fulton Public Library